BEGINNER'S GUIDE RIPPLE AFGHANS TO CROCHET

Ripples have been making waves in the world of crochet for years — Grandma kept a gorgeous ripple afghan in her favorite chair, and Aunt Ethel's was always on the back of the sofa. But you've steered clear of creating a ripple afghan because you thought you could only crochet in straight rows. Never fear — the truth is in here: **the ripple is one of the easiest patterns you can make!** In this Beginner's Guide to Ripple Afghans, we've put together the basics for fashioning this classic, and we've included **6 eye-catching designs** to encourage you to practice your skills. Our **easy-to-follow instructions** and **clear diagrams** will guide you to an understanding of the ripple technique, whether you're just learning how to crochet or you're an "experienced hand" at the craft! So get ready, get set, get stitching — **it's as easy as 1, 2, 3!**

HOW IS THE RIPPLE PATTERN CREATED?

You will be amazed at the simplicity of the ripple pattern. We've broken it into 3 easy steps. Take a look—

MAKE THE CHAIN. All ripple afghans, no matter how simple or intricate looking, begin with a crocheted chain.

USE INCREASES AND DECREASES TO ESTABLISH THE PATTERN. The first row starts the ripple pattern with evenly spaced increases and decreases. This creates the up and down pattern.

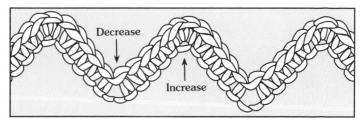

Decrease

Increase

© 1998 by Leisure Arts, Inc.
5701 Ranch Drive, Little Rock, AR 72223 **3**

CONTINUE THE ESTABLISHED PATTERN TO CREATE THE RIPPLE.

Every row is the same with the increases and decreases "stacked" over each other. Once you learn the pattern, you can work the ripple without even referring back to the instructions.

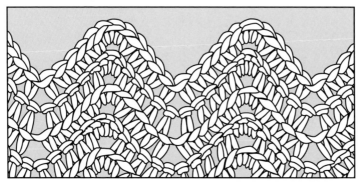

TRY IT YOURSELF!

Now that you have the concept, pick up some worsted weight yarn and a size H hook and let's try a swatch with a simple single crochet ripple.

Chain 66 loosely.

Work Row 1: Sc in third ch from hook and in next 4 chs, 3 sc in next ch *(this creates the "peak" of the ripple)*, ★ sc in the next 5 chs, skip next 2 chs *(this creates the "valley" of the ripple)*, sc in next 5 chs, 3 sc in next ch; repeat from ★ across to last 6 chs, sc in last 6 chs: 66 sc.

Work Rows 2-8: Ch 1, turn; working in Back Loops Only, skip first 2 sc, sc in next 5 sc, 3 sc in next sc *("peak")*, ★ sc in next 5 sc, skip next 2 sc *("valley")*, sc in next 5 sc, 3 sc in next sc; repeat from ★ across to last 6 sc, sc in last 6 sc.

Finish off.

Congratulations! You did it. Now pick one of our inspiring patterns and your favorite yarn and get started on your very own ripple afghan.

1. RAINBOW RIPPLE

Shown on page 1.

Finished Size:
47" x 60"

MATERIALS

Worsted Weight Yarn:
Color A (Pink) - 6 ounces,
(170 grams, 395 yards)
Color B (White) - 6 ounces,
(170 grams, 395 yards)
Color C (Peach) - 5 ounces,
(140 grams, 330 yards)
Color D (Yellow) - 5 ounces,
(140 grams, 330 yards)
Color E (Green) - 5 ounces,
(140 grams, 330 yards)
Color F (Blue) - 5 ounces,
(140 grams, 330 yards)
Color G (Lavender) - 5 ounces,
(140 grams, 330 yards)
Crochet hook, size I (5.50 mm)
or size needed for gauge

GAUGE: One repeat
from point to point = $5\frac{1}{4}$"
and 7 rows = $4\frac{1}{2}$"

Gauge Swatch:

$10\frac{1}{2}$"w x $4\frac{1}{2}$"h
Ch 51 **loosely**.
Work same as Afghan Body for
7 rows.
Finish off.

COLOR SEQUENCE

3 Rows Color A **(Fig. 7, page 19)**, one row Color B, ★ 3 rows Color C, one row Color B, 3 rows Color D, one row Color B, 3 rows Color E, one row Color B, 3 rows Color F, one row Color B, 3 rows Color G, one row Color B, 3 rows Color A, one row Color B; repeat from ★ 3 times **more**.

AFGHAN BODY

To work decrease (uses next 2 sts or sps), ★ YO, insert hook in **next** st or sp, YO and pull up a loop, YO and draw through 2 loops on hook; repeat from ★ once **more**, YO and draw through all 3 loops on hook **(counts as one dc)**.

To work V-St, (dc, ch 1, dc) in next st.

With Color A, ch 219 **loosely**.

Row 1 (Right side)**:** 2 Dc in fourth ch from hook **(3 skipped chs count as first dc)**, dc in next 8 chs, decrease, skip next 2 chs, decrease, dc in next 8 chs, ★ work V-St twice, dc in next 8 chs, decrease, skip next 2 chs, decrease, dc in next 8 chs; repeat from ★ across to last ch, 3 dc in last ch: 200 dc and 16 ch-1 sps.

Note: Mark last row as **right** side.

Rows 2 and 3: Ch 3 (counts as first dc, now and throughout), turn; 2 dc in same st, dc in next 8 dc, decrease, skip next 2 dc, decrease, ★ dc in next 7 dc and in next ch-1 sp, work V-St twice, dc in next ch-1 sp and in next 7 dc, decrease, skip next 2 dc, decrease; repeat from ★ across to last 9 dc, dc in next 8 dc, 3 dc in last dc.

Row 4: Ch 1, turn; sc in first dc, ch 1, (skip next dc, sc in next dc, ch 1) 4 times, skip next dc, sc in next 4 dc, ch 1, (skip next dc, sc in next dc, ch 1) 4 times, ★ skip next ch, sc in next 2 dc, ch 1, (skip next st, sc in next dc, ch 1) 4 times, skip next dc, sc in next 4 dc, ch 1, (skip next dc, sc in next dc, ch 1) 4 times; repeat from ★ across to last 2 dc, skip next dc, sc in last dc: 126 sc and 90 ch-1 sps.

Row 5: Ch 3, turn; 2 dc in same st, (dc in next ch-1 sp and in next sc) 4 times, decrease, skip next 2 sc, decrease, (dc in next sc and in next ch-1 sp) 4 times, ★ work V-St twice, (dc in next ch-1 sp and in next sc) 4 times, decrease, skip next 2 sc, decrease, (dc in next sc and in next ch-1 sp) 4 times; repeat from ★ across to last sc, 3 dc in last sc: 200 dc and 16 ch-1 sps.

Rows 6 and 7: Ch 3, turn; 2 dc in same st, dc in next 8 dc, decrease, skip next 2 dc, decrease, ★ dc in next 7 dc and in next ch-1 sp, work V-St twice, dc in next ch-1 sp and in next 7 dc, decrease, skip next 2 dc, decrease; repeat from ★ across to last 9 dc, dc in next 8 dc, 3 dc in last dc.

Rows 8-100: Repeat Rows 4-7, 23 times; then repeat Row 4 once **more**.

Finish off.

BOTTOM EDGING

Row 1: With **wrong** side facing and working in free loops of beginning ch *(Fig. 9, page 19)*, join Color B with slip st in first ch (at base of first 3 dc); ch 1, sc in same st, ch 1, (skip next ch, sc in next ch, ch 1) 4 times, skip next ch, (sc in next 2 chs, ch 1) twice, (skip next ch, sc in next ch, ch 1) 3 times, ★ skip next ch, sc in next 2 chs, skip next 2 chs, sc in next 2 chs, ch 1, (skip next ch, sc in next ch, ch 1) 3 times, skip next ch, (sc in next 2 chs, ch 1) twice, (skip next ch, sc in next ch, ch 1) 3 times; repeat from ★ across to last 4 chs, skip next ch, sc in next ch, ch 1, skip next ch, sc in last ch; finish off.

Design by Carole Prior.

2. PEACEFUL RIPPLE

Shown on page 2.

Finished Size:
48" x 65"

MATERIALS
Worsted Weight Yarn:
43 ounces,
(1,220 grams, 2,435 yards)
Crochet hook, size H (5.00 mm)
or size needed for gauge

GAUGE: In pattern, from point
to point = $4^3/_4$" and 8 rows = 4"

Gauge Swatch: $9^1/_2$"w x 4"h
Ch 41 **loosely.**
Work same as Afghan Body for
8 rows.
Finish off.

AFGHAN BODY
Ch 201 **loosely**.

Row 1: Sc in second ch from
hook and in next 9 chs, ch 2,
★ sc in next 9 chs, skip next 2
chs, sc in next 9 chs, ch 2;
repeat from ★ across to last 10
chs, sc in last 10 chs: 182 sc and
10 ch-2 sps.

*To work decrease (uses next 4
sc),* YO, insert hook in next sc,
YO and pull up a loop, YO and
draw through 2 loops on hook,
YO, skip next 2 sc, insert hook
in next sc, YO and pull up a
loop, YO and draw through 2
loops on hook, YO and draw
through all 3 loops on hook
(counts as one dc).

*To work ending decrease
(uses last 3 sc),* YO, insert hook
in next sc, YO and pull up a
loop, YO and draw through 2
loops on hook, YO, skip next sc,
insert hook in last sc, YO and
pull up a loop, YO and draw
through 2 loops on hook, YO
and draw through all 3 loops on
hook **(counts as one dc).**

Row 2 (Right side)**:** Ch 3
**(counts as first dc, now and
throughout),** turn; skip next sc,
(dc in next sc, ch 1, skip next sc)
4 times, (dc, ch 3, dc) in next
ch-2 sp, dc in next 7 sc,
★ decrease, ch 1, skip next sc,
(dc in next sc, ch 1, skip next sc)
3 times, (dc, ch 3, dc) in next
ch-2 sp, dc in next 7 sc; repeat
from ★ across to last 3 sc, work
ending decrease: 132 dc and 50
sps.

Row 3: Ch 1, turn; sc in first 9
dc, (sc, ch 2, sc) in next ch-3 sp,
(sc in next dc and in next ch-1
sp) 4 times, ★ skip next dc, sc in
next 8 dc, (sc, ch 2, sc) in next
ch-3 sp, (sc in next dc and in
next ch-1 sp) 4 times; repeat
from ★ across to last 2 dc, skip
next dc, sc in last dc: 182 sc and
10 ch-2 sps.

Rows 4-7: Repeat Rows 2 and 3 twice.

Row 8: Ch 3, turn; skip next sc, dc in next 8 sc, (dc, ch 3, dc) in next ch-2 sp, ch 1, (skip next sc, dc in next sc, ch 1) 3 times, ★ skip next sc, decrease, dc in next 7 sc, (dc, ch 3, dc) in next ch-2 sp, ch 1, (skip next sc, dc in next sc, ch 1) 3 times; repeat from ★ across to last 4 sc, skip next sc, work ending decrease: 132 dc and 50 sps.

Row 9: Ch 1, turn; sc in first dc, (sc in next ch-1 sp and in next dc) 4 times, (sc, ch 2, sc) in next ch-3 sp, sc in next 8 dc, ★ skip next dc, (sc in next ch-1 sp and in next dc) 4 times, (sc, ch 2, sc) in next ch-3 sp, sc in next 8 dc; repeat from ★ across to last 2 dc, skip next dc, sc in last dc: 182 sc and 10 ch-2 sps.

Rows 10-13: Repeat Rows 8 and 9 twice.

Rows 14-127: Repeat Rows 2-13, 9 times; then repeat Rows 2-7 once **more**.

EDGING

Ch 1, turn; slip st in first sc, ch 1, skip next sc, (slip st in next sc, ch 1, skip next sc) 4 times, (slip st, ch 1) twice in next ch-2 sp, ★ skip next sc, (slip st in next sc, ch 1, skip next sc) 3 times, slip st in next 4 sc, ch 1, skip next sc, (slip st in next sc, ch 1, skip next sc) 3 times, (slip st, ch 1) twice in next ch-2 sp; repeat from ★ across to last 10 sc, skip next sc, (slip st in next sc, ch 1, skip next sc) 4 times, (slip st, ch 1, slip st) in last sc, ch 3; working in end of rows, skip first 2 rows, slip st in next row, (ch 3, skip next row, slip st in next row) across, ch 2; working in free loops and in sps of beginning ch **(Fig. 9, page 19)**, slip st in ch at base of first sc, ch 1, skip next ch, (slip st in next ch, ch 1, skip next ch) 3 times, slip st in next 4 chs, † ch 1, skip next ch, (slip st in next ch, ch 1, skip next ch) 3 times, (slip st, ch 1) twice in next ch-2 sp, skip next ch, (slip st in next ch, ch 1, skip next ch) 3 times, slip st in next 4 chs †, repeat from † to † across to last 8 chs, (ch 1, skip next ch, slip st in next ch) 4 times, ch 2; working in end of rows, slip st in first row, ch 3, (skip next row, slip st in next row, ch 3) across to last 2 rows, skip last 2 rows, slip st in same st as first slip st, ch 1; join with slip st to first slip st, finish off.

Design by Anne Halliday.

3. FILET RIPPLES

Shown on page 22.

Finished Size:
48" x 62"

MATERIALS
Worsted Weight Yarn:
MC (Off-White) - 36 ounces,
(1,020 grams, 2,100 yards)
Color A (Green) - 12 ounces,
(340 grams, 700 yards)
Color B (Rose) - 10 ounces,
(280 grams, 585 yards)
Crochet hook, size P (10.00
mm) **or** size needed for gauge

Note: Entire Afghan is worked
holding 2 strands of yarn
together.

GAUGE: 7 dc = 3";
In pattern, one repeat = 6"
and 6 rows = 7"

Gauge Swatch: 12"w x 7"h
Ch 37 **loosely.**
Work same as Afghan Body for
6 rows.
Finish off.

AFGHAN BODY
COLOR SEQUENCE
4 Rows MC *(Fig. 7, page 19)*,
★ 1 row Color A, 1 row Color
B, 4 rows MC; repeat from ★
throughout.

*To work decrease (uses next 5
sts)*, YO, † insert hook in **next**
st, YO and pull up a loop, YO
and draw through 2 loops on
hook †, YO, skip next 3 sts,
repeat from † to † once, YO and
draw through all 3 loops on
hook **(counts as one dc).**

With MC, ch 157 **loosely.**

Row 1: Dc in fifth ch from
hook **(4 skipped chs count as
first dc plus ch 1)**, ch 1, (skip
next ch, dc in next ch, ch 1)
twice, skip next ch, (dc, ch 3, dc)
in next ch, ★ ch 1, (skip next ch,
dc in next ch, ch 1) 3 times, skip
next ch, decrease, ch 1, (skip
next ch, dc in next ch, ch 1) 3
times, skip next ch, (dc, ch 3, dc)
in next ch; repeat from ★ across
to last 6 chs, ch 1, (skip next ch,
dc in next ch, ch 1) twice, skip
next ch, (dc, ch 1, dc) in last ch:
73 dc.

*To work beginning decrease
(uses first 3 sts)*, ch 2, turn; skip
first 2 sts, dc in next dc **(counts
as one dc).**

*To work ending decrease
(uses last 3 sts)*, YO, † insert
hook in **next** st, YO and pull up
a loop, YO and draw through 2
loops on hook †, YO, skip next
st, repeat from † to † once, YO
and draw through all 3 loops on
hook **(counts as one dc).**

Row 2 (Right side)**:** Work beginning decrease, (dc in next ch-1 sp and in next dc) 3 times, (2 dc, ch 3, 2 dc) in next ch-3 sp, (dc in next dc and in next ch-1 sp) 3 times, ★ decrease, (dc in next ch-1 sp and in next dc) 3 times, (2 dc, ch 3, 2 dc) in next ch-3 sp, (dc in next dc and in next ch-1 sp) 3 times; repeat from ★ across to last 2 dc, work ending decrease: 137 dc.

Note: Mark last row as **right** side.

Row 3: Work beginning decrease, ch 1, (skip next dc, dc in next dc, ch 1) 3 times, (dc, ch 3, dc) in next ch-3 sp, ch 1, (dc in next dc, ch 1, skip next dc) 3 times, ★ decrease, ch 1, (skip next dc, dc in next dc, ch 1) 3 times, (dc, ch 3, dc) in next ch-3 sp, ch 1, (dc in next dc, ch 1, skip next dc) 3 times; repeat from ★ across to last 3 dc, work ending decrease: 73 dc.

Row 4: Work beginning decrease, (dc in next ch-1 sp and in next dc) 3 times, (2 dc, ch 3, 2 dc) in next ch-3 sp, (dc in next dc and in next ch-1 sp) 3 times, ★ decrease, (dc in next ch-1 sp and in next dc) 3 times, (2 dc, ch 3, 2 dc) in next ch-3 sp, (dc in next dc and in next ch-1 sp) 3 times; repeat from ★ across to last 2 dc, work ending decrease: 137 dc.

Rows 5-52: Repeat Rows 3 and 4, 24 times.

Finish off.

EDGING

With **right** side facing, join Color A with slip st in first dc; ch 1, sc in same st, skip next 2 dc, 5 dc in next dc, skip next 2 dc, sc in next dc, skip next 2 dc, 7 dc in next ch-3 sp, skip next 2 dc, sc in next dc, † (skip next 2 dc, 5 dc in next dc, skip next 2 dc, sc in next dc) twice, skip next 2 dc, 7 dc in next ch-3 sp, skip next 2 dc, sc in next dc †, repeat from † to † across to last 6 dc, skip next 2 dc, 5 dc in next dc, skip next 2 dc, sc in last dc; working in end of rows, (5 dc, sc) in first row, (5 dc in next row, sc in next row) across to last row, 7 dc in last row; working in unworked chs and in free loops of beginning ch *(Fig. 9, page 19)* and in ch-3 sps, sc in first ch, (skip next 2 chs, 5 dc in next ch, skip next 2 chs, sc in next ch) twice, ★ skip next 2 chs, 7 dc in next ch-3 sp, skip next 2 chs, sc in next ch, (skip next 2 chs, 5 dc in next ch, skip next 2 chs, sc in next ch) twice; repeat from ★ 6 times **more**; working in end of rows, 7 dc in first row, (sc in next row, 5 dc in next row) across to last row, (sc, 5 dc) in last row; join with slip st to first sc, finish off.

Design by Carole Prior.

4. LUXURIOUS RIPPLE

Shown on page 21.

Finished Size:
50" x 63"

MATERIALS

Worsted Weight Brushed Acrylic Yarn:
Sage - 29 ounces,
(820 grams, 1,835 yards)
Off-White - 13 ounces,
(370 grams, 825 yards)
Lavender - 13 ounces,
(370 grams, 825 yards)
Crochet hook, size N (9.00 mm) **or** size needed for gauge

GAUGE: In pattern, one repeat (16 sts) and 5 rows = 5"

Gauge Swatch: 10"w x 6"h
With Sage, ch 35 **loosely**.
Work same as Afghan Body for 6 rows.
Finish off.

AFGHAN BODY
COLOR SEQUENCE

2 Rows **each**: Sage **(Fig. 7, page 19)**, ★ Off-White, Lavender, Sage; repeat from ★ throughout.

To work Shell, (2 dc, ch 1, 2 dc) in st indicated.

To work decrease (uses next 5 sts), ★ YO, insert hook in **next** st, YO and pull up a loop, YO and draw through 2 loops on hook; repeat from ★ 4 times **more**, YO and draw through all 6 loops on hook **(counts as one dc)**.

To work ending decrease (uses last 3 sts), ★ YO, insert hook in **next** st, YO and pull up a loop, YO and draw through 2 loops on hook; repeat from ★ 2 times **more**, YO and draw through all 4 loops on hook **(counts as one dc)**.

With Sage, ch 163 **loosely**.

Row 1: YO, insert hook in fourth ch from hook, YO and pull up a loop, YO and draw through 2 loops on hook, YO, insert hook in next ch, YO and pull up a loop, YO and draw through 2 loops on hook, YO and draw through all 3 loops on hook **(counts as first dc)**, dc in next 5 chs, work Shell in next ch, dc in next 5 chs, ★ decrease, dc in next 5 chs, work Shell in next ch, dc in next 5 chs; repeat from ★ across to last 3 chs, work ending decrease.

To work beginning decrease (uses first 3 dc), ch 3, turn; ★ YO, insert hook in **next** dc, YO and pull up a loop, YO and draw through 2 loops on hook; repeat from ★ once **more**, YO and draw through all 3 loops on hook **(counts as one dc)**.

Row 2 (Right side): Working in Back Loops Only *(Fig. 8, page 19)*, work beginning decrease, dc in next 5 dc, work Shell in next ch, dc in next 5 dc, ★ decrease, dc in next 5 dc, work Shell in next ch, dc in next 5 dc; repeat from ★ across to last 3 dc, work ending decrease.

Note: Mark last row as **right** side.

Row 3: Working in Front Loops Only, work beginning decrease, dc in next 5 dc, work Shell in next ch, dc in next 5 dc, ★ decrease, dc in next 5 dc, work Shell in next ch, dc in next 5 dc; repeat from ★ across to last 3 dc, work ending decrease.

Row 4: Working in Back Loops Only, work beginning decrease, dc in next 5 dc, work Shell in next ch, dc in next 5 dc, ★ decrease, dc in next 5 dc, work Shell in next ch, dc in next 5 dc; repeat from ★ across to last 3 dc, work ending decrease.

Repeat Rows 3 and 4 for pattern until Afghan Body measures 63", ending by working 2 Sage rows; finish off.

CLUSTER STRIPES

To work Cluster, ch 3, ★ YO twice, insert hook in st indicated, YO and pull up a loop, (YO and draw through 2 loops on hook) twice; repeat from ★ 3 times **more**, YO and draw through all 5 loops on hook.

With **right** side facing and working from bottom edge to top edge, join Sage with slip st in free loop of ch at base of first Shell on Row 1 *(Fig. 9, page 19)*; work Cluster in same st, slip st in free loop of ch at top of same Shell, ★ work Cluster in same st, slip st in free loop of ch on Shell in next row; repeat from ★ to top edge; finish off.

Repeat along each column of Shells.

Using Sage, add tassels to each point across each end of afghan as follows:
Cut a piece of cardboard 4" wide and 9" long. Wind a double strand of yarn around the cardboard lengthwise approximately 20 times. Cut an 18" length of yarn and insert it under all of the strands at the top of the cardboard; pull up **tightly** and tie securely. Leave the yarn ends long enough to attach the

tassel. Cut the yarn at the opposite end of the cardboard and then remove it *(Fig. A)*. Cut a 6" length of yarn and wrap it **tightly** around the tassel twice, 1" below the top *(Fig. B)*; tie securely. Trim the ends.

Design by Fran Marlin.

Fig. A

Fig. B

---

5. IRRESISTIBLE RIPPLES
Shown on Front Cover.

Finished Size:
52" x 70"

MATERIALS
Worsted Weight Yarn:
Color A (Dk Blue) - 8 ounces, (230 grams, 525 yards)
Color B (Med Blue) - 13 ounces, (370 grams, 855 yards)
Color C (Lt Blue) - 13 ounces, (370 grams, 855 yards)
Color D (Ecru) - 7 ounces, (200 grams, 460 yards)
Crochet hook, size I (5.50 mm) **or** size needed for gauge

GAUGE: In pattern, 2 repeats = 8½" and 8 rows = 4½"

Gauge Swatch: 8½"w x 4½"h
Ch 51 **loosely**.
Work same as Afghan Body for 8 rows.
Finish off.

COLOR SEQUENCE
2 Rows **each**: Color A, ★ Color B, Color C, Color D, Color C, Color B, Color A; repeat from ★ 9 times **more**.

AFGHAN BODY
To work Cluster, pull up a loop in next 3 chs, YO and draw through all 4 loops on hook.

To work decrease, pull up a loop in next 6 chs, YO and draw through all 7 loops on hook.

With Color A, ch 291 **loosely**.

Row 1: Insert hook in third ch from hook, YO and pull up a loop, pull up a loop in next 2 chs, YO and draw through all 4 loops on hook, (ch 3, work Cluster) 3 times, ch 6, (work Cluster, ch 3) 3 times,

13

★ decrease, (ch 3, work Cluster) 3 times, ch 6, (work Cluster, ch 3) 3 times; repeat from ★ across to last 4 chs, work Cluster, hdc in last ch.

Note: Work in Back Loops Only throughout *(Fig. 8, page 19)*.

Row 2 (Right side)**:** Ch 2, turn; skip first Cluster, work Cluster, (ch 3, skip next Cluster, work Cluster) 3 times, ch 6, (work Cluster, ch 3, skip next Cluster) 3 times, ★ decrease, (ch 3, skip next Cluster, work Cluster) 3 times, ch 6, (work Cluster, ch 3, skip next Cluster) 3 times; repeat from ★ across to last ch-3 sp, work Cluster, skip next Cluster, hdc in top of beginning ch; finish off.

Note: Mark last row as **right** side.

Row 3: With **wrong** side facing, join next color with slip st in first hdc; ch 2, skip first Cluster, work Cluster, (ch 3, skip next Cluster, work Cluster) 3 times, ch 6, (work Cluster, ch 3, skip next Cluster) 3 times, ★ decrease, (ch 3, skip next Cluster, work Cluster) 3 times, ch 6, (work Cluster, ch 3, skip next Cluster) 3 times; repeat from ★ across to last ch-3 sp, work Cluster, skip next Cluster, hdc in top of beginning ch; do **not** finish off.

Row 4: Ch 2, turn; skip first Cluster, work Cluster, (ch 3, skip next Cluster, work Cluster) 3 times, ch 6, (work Cluster, ch 3, skip next Cluster) 3 times, ★ decrease, (ch 3, skip next Cluster, work Cluster) 3 times, ch 6, (work Cluster, ch 3, skip next Cluster) 3 times; repeat from ★ across to last ch-3 sp, work Cluster, skip next Cluster, hdc in top of beginning ch; finish off.

Rows 5-122: Repeat Rows 3 and 4, 59 times; at end of Row 122, do **not** finish off.

EDGING

Ch 1, do **not** turn; working in end of rows, slip st in first row, ch 1, (slip st in next row, ch 1) across to last row, (slip st, ch 3, slip st) in last row; working in sp between Clusters, (ch 3, slip st in next sp) 3 times, (ch 1, slip st in next sp) twice, ch 3, (slip st in next sp, ch 3) twice, † (slip st, ch 3, slip st) in center of next decrease, (ch 3, slip st in next sp) 3 times, (ch 1, slip st in next sp) twice, ch 3, (slip st in next sp, ch 3) twice †, repeat from † to †

10 times **more**; working in end of rows, (slip st, ch 3, slip st) in first row, (ch 1, slip st in next row) across, ch 3; slip st in first ch-3 sp, ch 3, (slip st in next ch-3 sp, ch 3) twice, (slip st, ch 3) twice in next ch-6 sp, ★ (slip st in next ch-3 sp, ch 3) 6 times, (slip st, ch 3) twice in next ch-6 sp; repeat from ★ 10 times **more**, (slip st in next ch-3 sp, ch 3) 3 times; join with slip st to first st, finish off.

Design by Anne Halliday.

---

6. RUSTIC RIPPLE
Shown on page 20.

Finished Size:
48" x 60"

MATERIALS
Worsted Weight Yarn:
MC (Ecru) - 31 ounces,
(880 grams, 1,950 yards)
Color A (Green) - 12 ounces,
(340 grams, 755 yards)
Color B (Rust) - 12 ounces,
(340 grams, 755 yards)
Crochet hook, size P (10.00 mm)
or size needed for gauge

Note: Afghan is worked holding two strands of yarn together.

GAUGE: In pattern,
2 repeats = 16" and 4 rows = 4"

Gauge Swatch: 16"w x 4"h
Ch 40 **loosely**.
Work same as Afghan for 4 rows.

AFGHAN
With MC, ch 116 **loosely**.

Row 1 (Right side)**:** Dc in fifth ch from hook and in next 6 chs, (dc, ch 2, dc) in next ch, ★ dc in next 8 chs, skip next 2 chs, dc in next 8 chs, (dc, ch 2, dc) in next ch; repeat from ★ across to last 9 chs, dc in next 7 chs, skip next ch, dc in last ch.

Note: Mark last row as **right** side.

Row 2: Ch 3 **(counts as first dc, now and throughout)**, turn; skip next dc, dc in next 7 dc, (dc, ch 2, dc) in next ch-2 sp, ★ dc in next 8 dc, skip next 2 dc, dc in next 8 dc, (dc, ch 2, dc) in next ch-2 sp; repeat from ★ across to last 9 sts, dc in next 7 dc, skip next dc, dc in next ch: 108 dc.

Rows 3 and 4: Ch 3, turn; skip next dc, dc in next 7 dc, (dc, ch 2, dc) in next ch-2 sp, ★ dc in next 8 dc, skip next 2 dc, dc in next 8 dc, (dc, ch 2, dc) in next ch-2 sp; repeat from ★ across to last 9 dc, dc in next 7 dc, skip next dc, dc in last dc; at end of Row 4, finish off.

Row 5: With **right** side facing, join Color A with slip st in first dc; ch 3, skip next dc, dc in next 7 dc, (dc, ch 2, dc) in next ch-2 sp, ★ dc in next 8 dc, skip next 2 dc, dc in next 8 dc, (dc, ch 2, dc) in next ch-2 sp; repeat from ★ across to last 9 dc, dc in next 7 dc, skip next dc, dc in last dc; finish off.

Row 6: With **wrong** side facing, join Color B with slip st in first dc; ch 3, skip next dc, dc in next 7 dc, (dc, ch 2, dc) in next ch-2 sp, ★ dc in next 8 dc, skip next 2 dc, dc in next 8 dc, (dc, ch 2, dc) in next ch-2 sp; repeat from ★ across to last 9 dc, dc in next 7 dc, skip next dc, dc in last dc.

Row 7: Ch 3, turn; skip next dc, dc in next 7 dc, (dc, ch 2, dc) in next ch-2 sp, ★ dc in next 8 dc, skip next 2 dc, dc in next 8 dc, (dc, ch 2, dc) in next ch-2 sp; repeat from ★ across to last 9 dc, dc in next 7 dc, skip next dc, dc in last dc; finish off.

Row 8: With **wrong** side facing, join Color A with slip st in first dc; ch 3, skip next dc, dc in next 7 dc, (dc, ch 2, dc) in next ch-2 sp, ★ dc in next 8 dc, skip next 2 dc, dc in next 8 dc, (dc, ch 2, dc) in next ch-2 sp; repeat from ★ across to last 9 dc, dc in next 7 dc, skip next dc, dc in last dc; finish off.

Row 9: With **right** side facing, join MC with slip st in first dc; ch 3, skip next dc, dc in next 7 dc, (dc, ch 2, dc) in next ch-2 sp, ★ dc in next 8 dc, skip next 2 dc, dc in next 8 dc, (dc, ch 2, dc) in next ch-2 sp; repeat from ★ across to last 9 dc, dc in next 7 dc, skip next dc, dc in last dc.

Rows 10-12: Ch 3, turn; skip next dc, dc in next 7 dc, (dc, ch 2, dc) in next ch-2 sp, ★ dc in next 8 dc, skip next 2 dc, dc in next 8 dc, (dc, ch 2, dc) in next ch-2 sp; repeat from ★ across to last 9 dc, dc in next 7 dc, skip next dc, dc in last dc; at end of Row 12, finish off.

Rows 13-60: Repeat Rows 5-12, 6 times.

Design by Terry Kimbrough.

GENERAL INSTRUCTIONS

ABBREVIATIONS

ch(s)	chain(s)
dc	double crochet(s)
hdc	half double crochet(s)
MC	Main Color
mm	millimeters
sc	single crochet(s)
sp(s)	space(s)
st(s)	stitch(es)
YO	yarn over

★ — work instructions following ★ as many **more** times as indicated in addition to the first time.

† to † — work all instructions from first † to second † **as many** times as specified.

( ) or [ ] — work enclosed instructions **as many** times as specified by the number immediately following **or** work all enclosed instructions in the stitch or space indicated **or** contains explanatory remarks.

colon (:) — the number(s) given after a colon at the end of a row or round denote(s) the number of stitches you should have on that row or round.

GAUGE

Exact gauge is **essential** for proper size. Before beginning your project, make the sample swatch given in the individual instructions in the yarn and hook specified. After completing the swatch, measure it, counting your stitches and rows carefully. If your swatch is larger or smaller than specified, **make another, changing hook size to get the correct gauge**. Keep trying until you find the size hook that will give you the specified gauge.

ALUMINUM CROCHET HOOKS	
UNITED STATES	**METRIC (mm)**
B-1	2.25
C-2	2.75
D-3	3.25
E-4	3.50
F-5	3.75
G-6	4.00
H-8	5.00
I-9	5.50
J-10	6.00
K-10½	6.50
N	9.00
P	10.00
Q	15.00

CROCHET TERMINOLOGY	
UNITED STATES	**INTERNATIONAL**
slip stitch (slip st)	= single crochet (sc)
single crochet (sc)	= double crochet (dc)
half double crochet (hdc)	= half treble crochet (htr)
double crochet (dc)	= treble crochet (tr)
treble crochet (tr)	= double treble crochet (dtr)
double treble crochet (dtr)	= triple treble crochet (ttr)
skip	= miss

CHAIN

To work a chain stitch, begin with a slip knot on the hook. Bring the yarn **over** hook from back to front, catching the yarn with the hook and turning the hook slightly toward you to keep the yarn from slipping off. Draw the yarn through the slip knot **(Fig. 1) (first chain st made, *abbreviated ch)*.**

Fig. 1

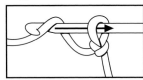

WORKING INTO THE CHAIN

When counting chains, always begin with the first chain from the hook and then count toward the beginning of your foundation chain **(Fig. 2a)**.

Fig. 2a

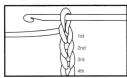

Method 1: Insert hook under top two strands of each chain **(Fig. 2b)**.

Fig. 2b

Method 2: Insert hook into back ridge of each chain **(Fig. 2c)**.

Fig. 2c

SLIP STITCH

To work a slip stitch, insert hook in st or sp indicated, YO and draw through st and through loop on hook **(Fig. 3) (slip stitch made, *abbreviated slip st)*.**

Fig. 3

SINGLE CROCHET

Insert hook in st or sp indicated, YO and pull up a loop, YO and draw through both loops on hook **(Fig. 4) (single crochet made, *abbreviated sc)*.**

Fig. 4

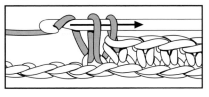

We have made every effort to ensure that these instructions are accurate and complete. We cannot, however, be responsible for human error, typographical mistakes, or variations in individual work.

HALF DOUBLE CROCHET

YO, insert hook in st or sp indicated, YO and pull up a loop, YO and draw through all 3 loops on hook *(Fig. 5)* **(half double crochet made,** *abbreviated hdc)*.

Fig. 5

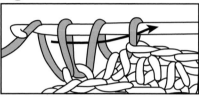

DOUBLE CROCHET

YO, insert hook in st or sp indicated, YO and pull up a loop, YO and draw through 2 loops on hook *(Fig. 6a)*, YO and draw through remaining 2 loops on hook *(Fig. 6b)* **(double crochet made,** *abbreviated dc)*.

Fig. 6a

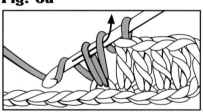

Fig. 6b

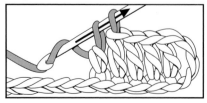

CHANGING COLORS

Work the last stitch to within one step of completion, hook new yarn *(Fig. 7)* and draw through all loops on hook. Cut old yarn and work over both ends.

Fig. 7

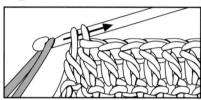

BACK OR FRONT LOOP ONLY

Work only in loop(s) indicated by arrow *(Fig. 8)*.

Fig. 8

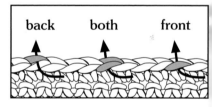

back   both   front

FREE LOOPS OF A CHAIN

When instructed to work in free loops of a chain, work in loop indicated by arrow *(Fig. 9)*.

Fig. 9

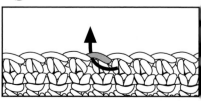